3 1994 01321 0221

SANTA ANA PUBLIC LIBRARY

2/06

D1505680

FIGHTING FORCES ON THE SEA

COAST GUARD CUTTERS

J 623.8263 STO
Stone, Lynn M.
Coast Guard cutters

CENTRAL $28.50
                    31994013210221

LYNN M. STONE

Rourke

Publishing LLC
Vero Beach, Florida 32964

© 2006 Rourke Publishing LLC

All rights reserved. No part of this book may be reproduced or utilized in any form or by any means, electronic or mechanical including photocopying, recording, or by any information storage and retrieval system without permission in writing from the publisher.

www.rourkepublishing.com

PHOTO CREDITS: p. 22, 23 courtesy Naval Institute; p. 24, 25 courtesy U.S. Department of Defense National Archives; all other photos courtesy U.S. Coast Guard

Title page: *Patrolling off Key West, Florida, the medium endurance CGC Mohawk shows off the familiar red, white, and blue trim of USCG cutters.*

Editor: Frank Sloan

Library of Congress Cataloging-in-Publication Data

Stone, Lynn M.
  Coast Guard cutters / Lynn M. Stone.
    p. cm. -- (Fighting forces on the sea)
  Includes bibliographical references and index.
  ISBN 1-59515-462-0 (hardcover)

Printed in the USA

CG/CG

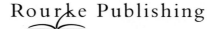
Rourke Publishing

www.rourkepublishing.com – sales@rourkepublishing.com
Post Office Box 3328, Vero Beach, FL 32964
1-800-394-7055

TABLE OF CONTENTS

CHAPTER ONE

COAST GUARD CUTTERS

U.S. Coast Guard cutters are vessels over 65 feet (20 meters) in length and with enough live-aboard space for the vessel's crew. That definition covers a broad range of vessels. The longest cutter, the 420-foot (128-meter) USCGC (United States Coast Guard Cutter) *Healy*, is 6-1/2 times the length of the smallest vessels—the three types of 65-foot (20-meter) long cutters used as river **buoy** tenders, inland buoy tenders, and small harbor tugs.

The largest of Coast Guard cutters, the cutter Healy, *is a polar icebreaker and research vessel and has many other capabilities.*

The CGC Midgett is the 12th and last of the Coast Guard's fleet of 378-foot (115-meter) long high endurance cutters.

Some of the vessels the Coast Guard lists as cutters go strictly by that name. There are, for example, high endurance cutters and medium endurance cutters. But many vessels the Coast Guard lists as cutters also have more specific names: icebreaker, seagoing buoy tender, inland construction tender, coastal patrol boat, and others. The Coast Guard lumps together some 25 different types or sizes of vessels as cutters. Vessels under 65 feet (20 meters) in length are considered boats.

▲

Big coastal buoy tenders, like the Joshua Appleby *shown here, are classed as USCGC, or cutters. The 175-foot (53-meter) long* Appleby *is among the first cutters equipped with Z-drive propulsion for greater maneuverability.*

The word "cutter" has a long history in the Coast Guard. The Coast Guard's first 10 boats, launched in the 1790s, were called **revenue** cutters. They were relatively small, decked sailing ships. Although vessel design has changed dramatically, the Coast Guard tradition of using the name *cutter* goes on.

The U.S. Coast Guard is one of the nation's five military services. It has five missions centered on the activity of vessels using the seas and other large bodies of water. One of its missions is national defense. That includes homeland security, port and waterway security, and general defense. It is in this area that Coast Guard crews and cutters have traditionally become "fighting forces."

FACT FILE ★

INTERCEPTING ILLEGAL GOODS HAD BEEN A MAIN MISSION OF THE COAST GUARD BEFORE WORLD WAR II. DURING **PROHIBITION** (1920-1923) IN THE UNITED STATES, CUTTERS HAD THE RESPONSIBILITY OF STOPPING "RUM RUNNERS," BOATS THAT WERE SMUGGLING LIQUOR INTO THE UNITED STATES.

▲

The cutter Tampa, a 270-foot (82-meter) long medium endurance cutter, sails home after a 60-day law enforcement patrol.

Other Coast Guard missions include **maritime** safety, maritime security, maritime mobility, and the protection of natural **aquatic** resources.

Together, the Coast Guard missions involve education, lawmaking, law enforcement, military operations, research, and a host of other activities. A single cutter may be used for several different purposes. The USCGC *Healy*, for example, is more than an icebreaker. It has huge laboratory spaces and room for 50 scientists aboard.

FACT FILE ★

AS PART OF ITS MARITIME SECURITY MISSION, THE COAST GUARD ENFORCES U.S. AND INTERNATIONAL FISHERIES LAWS. THE U.S. HAS A PRIVATE **COMMERCIAL** FISHING ZONE WITHIN 200 MILES (320 KILOMETERS) OF ITS ROUGHLY 95,000 MILES (152,000 KILOMETERS) OF SEACOAST. PART OF THE COAST GUARD'S JOB IS TO PROTECT THAT **EXCLUSIVE** FISHING ZONE AGAINST FISHING FLEETS FROM OTHER NATIONS.

Polar cutters are homes away from home for scientists who work in both Arctic and Antarctic environments.

Maritime mobility is a mission in which the Coast Guard provides aids to navigation, performs icebreaking services, provides and enforces navigation rules, and provides bridge administration.

Finally, the Coast Guard is charged with protecting natural resources. In that capacity, it provides marine pollution education and enforcement of laws, oversees protection of natural aquatic resources, and works with marine and environmental science projects and scientists. The *Healy* and *Polar Star*, for instance, are equipped with multiple laboratories for scientists. They are also outfitted for search and rescue, ship escort, environmental protection, and law enforcement duties.

CUTTER SPECIFICATIONS

Hamilton class
High Endurance Cutter (WHEC)

Powerplant:
2 diesel engines, 2 gas turbine engines

Length:
378 feet (115 meters)

Beam:
43 feet (13 meters)

Displacement:
3,250 tons (2,958 metric tons), fully loaded

Speed:
28+ knots (32+ miles, 51+ kilometers per hour)

Aircraft:
1 HH-60J Jayhawk helicopter

Ship's company:
178

Armament:
1 76mm OTO compact DP gun, 1 20mm Phalanx Close-In Weapons System, 2 25mm Bushmaster low-angle guns, 4 12.7mm machine guns

Commissioning date, first ship:
1967

Famous class
Medium Endurance Patrol Cutter (WMEC)

Powerplant:
2 diesel engines

Length:
270 feet (82 meters)

Beam:
38 feet (11.6 meters)

Displacement:
1,825 tons (1,661 metric tons)

Speed:
19 knots (22 miles, 35 kilometers per hour)

Aircraft:
1 HH-60J Jayhawk or HH-65A helicopter

Ship's company:
100

Armament:
1 76mm OTO compact DP gun, 2 12.7mm machine guns

Commissioning date, first ship:
1983

The cutter Narwhal *speeds along the southern California coast during a law enforcement patrol.*

CHAPTER TWO

CUTTER CHARACTERISTICS

Coast Guard cutters are easy to recognize. They wear a handsome coat of either red or white and the Coast Guard shield. But beyond the paint, the cutters are a mixed bag of vessels!

◄ *The cutter* Polar Star *knifes through an Antarctic ice pack on one of her primary missions, the support of America's McMurdo Research Station in the frozen Ross Sea.*

The wide-bodied *Healy*—it is 82 feet (25 meters) across—is the Coast Guard's largest ship. If compared to the U.S. Navy's guided missile cruisers and destroyers in water **displacement**, the *Healy* is bigger (with a displacement of 16,000 tons, 14,560 metric tons)! As an icebreaker, the *Healy* can steadily ram through 4-1/2 feet (1.4 meters) of ice at a speed of 3 knots (3.5 miles, 5.5 kilometers per hour) and operate in temperatures as low as -50 degrees Fahrenheit (-45.5 degrees Celsius).

▲
The Healy *smashes through Arctic ice. The cutter was named for Captain Michael A. Healy, who piloted the U.S. Revenue Service cutter* Bear *from 1886 to 1895, often in the frigid Bering Sea.*

▲

A veteran of World War II patrols, the Storis, *photographed here in her home port of Kodiak, Alaska, reigns as the "Queen of the Fleet" in the modern U.S. Coast Guard.*

Another of the Coast Guard's most storied ships is the 230-foot (70-meter) long Arctic patrol cutter *Storis*. She was built in wartime 1942 for patrol and icebreaking around Greenland. The *Storis* continues to prowl cold seas, near Kodiak, Alaska. She is the oldest cutter in service.

Except for the three big icebreaking cutters, the 378-foot (115-meter) long high endurance cutters are the largest ships ever built for the Coast Guard. In length and displacement, the 12 high endurance ships are about four-fifths the size of the Navy's guided missile frigates, which the big, sleek cutters resemble.

High endurance cutters are what the Coast Guard and Navy call "blue water capable," which means they can comfortably operate on the deep, open oceans.

▲
The high endurance cutter Dallas *escorts a Spanish vessel carrying four U.S. Coast Guard patrol boats to the Mediterranean in support of Operation Enduring Freedom.*

▲

An HH-60 Jayhawk helicopter practices a hoist rescue along the cliffs of Kodiak Island, Alaska.

Many of the larger cutters can carry an HH-60J Jayhawk or HH-65A Dolphin helicopter. As a flying arm of the ship, a helicopter helps extend a cutter's "view" of its surroundings. Helicopters are important tools, too, in search and rescue, law enforcement, and homeland security.

Despite their comparable size to the Navy's frigate warships, cutters are not designed for naval warfare, so they are not heavily armed. They do, however, carry several different weapons, including a variety of machine guns and the Phalanx Close-In Weapons System, built around 20-millimeter guns. Cutters have enough firepower to stop any merchant ship by force, if necessary.

▲

An MK-75 Oto Melara 76-millimeter gun points from its mount on a high endurance cutter. Linked to the MK-92 Fire Control System, it can fire 80 rounds in one minute.

CHAPTER THREE

In its in infancy, the service that became the U.S. Coast Guard was the Revenue Cutter Service. It was created at the request of Secretary of the Treasury Alexander Hamilton. Hamilton wanted a fleet of small, fast ships to help stamp out piracy and smuggling along the U.S. Atlantic coast.

Beginning in the 1790s and continuing well into the 1800s, revenue cutters were ordered to intercept ships carrying slaves from Africa as well as combat pirates. The cutters *Alabama* and *Louisiana* captured pirate Jean LaFarge's *Bravo* in 1819.

▲

The United States Revenue Service cutter Louis McLane *was built as a commercial steamship. She became a USRC cutter in 1865.*

Cutters fought British vessels along the American coast in the War of 1812 (1812-1815). Cutters were used to attack, drop off soldiers, pick up warfare survivors, carry messages, and **blockade** rivers.

By the time the United States had entered World War I (1914-1918) in April, 1917, the Revenue Cutter Service had been joined with other maritime services as the U.S. Coast Guard. As provided by U.S. law, the Coast Guard was put under control of the U.S. Navy as America entered the war. Six cutters were sent to Europe. One of them, *Tampa*, was sunk, probably by a German submarine's torpedoes, in September, 1918, with the loss of its entire crew—115 men.

▲
The USRC McCulloch, a steamship with sails, entered service in 1897 and continued into World War I.

WORLD WAR II

Again in World War II (1939-1945), the Coast Guard operated as part of the Navy. More than 800 cutters were active both along American coasts and in foreign waters as well. They were on constant patrol at home, watching for **saboteurs** and German submarines. And when submarines struck, the cutters were life-savers. Cutters and other USCG craft rescued more than 1,500 survivors of torpedo attacks near the United States.

▲

Two coastguardsmen scrape oil from a survivor of the USS Lansdale, *an American destroyer sunk by German planes off the coast of North Africa in April, 1944.*

Coast Guardsmen aboard the cutter Spencer *watch one of the cutter's depth charges explode. On April 17, 1943, the* Spencer *destroyed the German submarine* U-175.

Overseas, cutters on escort duty saved more than 1,000 lives. During the D-Day invasion of France, which began on June 6, 1944, cutters and their crews braved mines and German shore fire to save hundreds of Allied soldiers from the sea. More than 600 Coast Guardsmen died in combat during World War II.

CHAPTER FIVE

In 1965, as U.S. military forces in Vietnam rapidly grew, 26 cutters were sent to intercept Vietcong and North Vietnamese troops and small boats in **riverine** and coastal areas. This was the so-called "brown water" war, named for the sometimes muddy rivers and coastal waters. By the end of American involvement in Vietnam, 56 cutters had served in the conflict.

After the terrorist attacks in New York City on September 11, 2001, the Coast Guard became part of the new Department of Homeland Security in 2003. Cutters were sent to Iraqi waters later that year to assist in naval operations during Operation Iraqi Freedom.

FACT FILE

CUTTERS HAVE BEEN WIDELY USED IN THE SEAS BETWEEN CUBA AND FLORIDA BOTH TO ENFORCE IMMIGRATION AND ARMS LAWS AND TO ASSIST IN LEGAL IMMIGRATION FROM CUBA TO THE UNITED STATES. DURING THE MARIEL BOATLIFT OF 1980, CUTTERS HELPED MORE THAN 125,000 CUBANS MAKE SAFE LANDINGS IN FLORIDA.

Helicopters like the Jayhawk work hand in hand with Coast Guard cutters to patrol a massive expanse of sea.

CHAPTER SIX

Coast Guard cutters had a huge job in policing more than 95,000 miles (152,000 kilometers) of U.S. coastline and 3.5 million square miles (9.1 million square kilometers) of ocean even before September 11, 2001. With the threat of future terrorism, the Coast Guard's military job has become even bigger—and more important.

The Coast Guard hopes to improve its ability to deal with homeland threats and its other missions, in part, through the Deepwater Program. Among other things, this plan is designed to modernize many current cutters. It will also introduce three new classes of cutters, upgraded helicopters, and unmanned aerial vehicles, some of them cutter-based. The Coast Guard takes its Latin motto, *Semper Paratus*—"always ready"—seriously.

Modern cutters and their helicopter companions help keep the Coast Guard "always ready."

GLOSSARY

aquatic (uh KWAT ik) — of or relating to water

blockade (blaw KAID) — a ship or group of ships organized to prevent goods from reaching a destination by sea or river

buoy (BOO ee) — a floating device anchored in a waterway to warn vessels of danger

commercial (kuh MUR shul) — of or relating to trade or commerce

displacement (dis PLAY smunt) — the water displaced by a floating ship; the tonnage of the water displaced

exclusive (eks KLU siv) — referring to single ownership; that which is reserved for private use

maritime (MARE uh TIME) — of or relating to the sea or sea commerce

Prohibition (PRO uh BISH un) — to forbid, by law, the making, transport, and sale of beverages containing alcohol

revenue (REV uh NYU) — monies collected

riverine (RIV uh REEN) — of or relating to rivers

saboteurs (SAB uh TURZ) — those who would act to undermine or sabotage; those who conduct secret, destructive missions

INDEX

FURTHER READING

Braulick, Carrie A. *U.S. Coast Guard*. Blazers, 2005
Cooper, Jason. *U.S. Coast Guard*. Rourke, 2000
Noble, Dennis L. *The U.S. Coast Guard*. Gareth Stevens,
     2005

WEBSITES TO VISIT

http://www.uscg.mil/USCG.shtm
http://www.uscg.mil/datasheet/dataindx.htm

ABOUT THE AUTHOR

Lynn M. Stone is the author and photographer of many children's
books. Lynn is a former teacher who travels worldwide to pursue
his varied interests.